Morning Does Come

Sophie Haworth

BookLeaf Publishing

India | USA | UK

Morning Does Come © 2022 Sophie Haworth

All rights reserved.

No part of this publication may be reproduced, stored in a retrieval system, or transmitted, in any form or by any means, electronic, mechanical, photocopying, recording or otherwise, without the prior written permission of the presenters.

Sophie Haworth asserts the moral right to be identified as author of this work.

Presentation by *BookLeaf Publishing*

Web: www.bookleafpub.com

E-mail: info@bookleafpub.com

ISBN: 9789357446488

First edition 2022

To people who miss those who are not here.

One

Creaking floorboards underfoot.
Each step brings up dust,
From between the ancient knots;
Created centuries past.
To know they once were
Faerie doors to distant lands.
Dried herbs hang above the door;
Scents of lavender
And rosemary combining.
Tied together by twine,
Smudge sticks granting peace;
They will bring tranquility.
She turns off the lights,
Leaving the store in darkness.
Luna locks the door
Not a single ghost to haunt,
The dead now sleeping,
All the living: warm inside.
So quiet are the nights, now.
Wind whistles through trees.
Amber leaves fall like glitter.
Owls hoot from high above,
Searching for some prey.
The witch wishes them luck.
A heavy sigh from her comes

Her gaze turned to stars.
If only she were elsewhere.

Two

Her room was lit up by the moon.
Her tired eyes that wouldn't sleep.
How she wishes dawn will come soon.

Her phone held pictures from last June
When they all made promises they could not
keep.
Her room was lit up by the moon.

Luna had thought she'd be immune,
From the loneliness that ran deep.
How she wishes dawn will come soon.

The witch's emotions swirl in a typhoon;
Sadness and envy that make her weep.
Her room was lit up by the moon.

Memories with old friends lay strewn,
But in her mind they creep.
How she wishes dawn will come soon.

She's seen the fun they had so soon;
Left her behind for darkness to seep.
Her room was lit up by the moon;
How she wishes dawn will come soon.

Three

There is a young guy named Pan,
They now work with the baker man.
Luna soon saw,
With her hand on the door,
And a friendship then began.

Four

The park is quiet,
With no other soul in sight.
Just Luna and Pan.

They talk about life,
And let true friendship begin.
Just Luna and Pan.

The moon is so full,
Shining down upon the pair.
Just Luna and Pan.

Five

Bright lights hang in the sky,
Hung from string to guide the way.
Bustling crowds bring screams of joy.
Look to the swinging ferris wheel,
Creaking as it goes round and round.
Time to wait in queues, for
Hot chocolates, doughnuts, and candyfloss.
Win a teddy bear at hook the duck,
Or a pack of water guns and a glittery Barbie.
All these smiles just hit different at night.

'Luna's smile just hits different at night'
So Pan thinks, looking back to their past.
Pan wins her a stuffed unicorn at hook the duck,
And laughs at the sugar coating her chin.
Her smile just hits different at night.
Pan hopes this friendship will forever last.
It seems like laughter will never die,
As bustling crowds bring screams of joy
They look to the stars that feel like fate.
Bright lights hang in the sky.

Bright lights hang in the sky.
They sparkle in Pan's eyes;
To Luna they are stars in dark nothing,

A beacon of hope from past loneliness.
Luna hopes this friendship will forever last.
It seems like laughter will never die,
Even when she fails at hook the duck,
Because Pan is there, holding out a unicorn.
Both seeming impossible, yet both right there.
These smiles just hit different at night.

Six

Amber leaves, from trees,
Litter the ground like wildfire;
Too damp to catch light.

Puffs of air like clouds.
Scarves wrapped tight around their necks.
The chilly air seeps.

Look! Will-o-the-wisps.
They guide travellers through dark,
Never-ending woods.

Luna clasps Pan's hand,
Their arms swinging between them.
Smiles beam; supernova.

A clearing appears.
Townspeople clutch hot chocolate flasks,
Singing to the fire.

Tiny flickers like sparks
Dance around the tears on cheeks;
Glistening; Shining.

Luna turns to Pan,

Explains the magical sight
Of midnight fairies

Only found at night,
The fire always burning,
At dawn: out of sight.

Seven

It was a snowy night.
Clear ice on unsalted roads.
If only it had showed
Up under the headlights.

It was a horrid sight
For the passing car that slowed;
A sorrow we cannot decode,
Like fate was full of spite

Metal scratched against metal.
A door smashed around a tree.
Something goes *drip drip drip*

Bright red like a rose petal,
A horror they could not foresee,
Pan's blood goes *drip drip drip*

Eight

Fingers clasped so tight around
A phone with a shattered screen.
Her knuckles burn so
White.
The news sends bruises
Up bare arms. The darkness
Behind closed eyes, so
Black.
The hospital halls never
End, her aching heart needs
Release. She collapses on floors so
White.
A friction burn on weak
Knees. She is too numb to feel the
Pain. But her eyes do widen at blood so
Red.

Nine

Mourners like ravens;
Black from head to toe.
Only three people stand
In the sleet. Umbrellas held
Up above them. All their
Eyes are puffy.
Luna, her mum, and the baker man.
Only two grab a handful of
Soil, to drop atop the coffin.
For Luna turns away, her
Face scrunched in fury, and
Fear, and grief.
She cannot say goodbye.
She cannot be abandoned again.
She cannot admit she is alone.

Ten

Curse the stars
The night
The snow
The cars.

Curse the smiles
The unicorns
The doughnuts
The childs.

Curse the Will-o-the-wisps
The fairies
The bonfire
The life that is missed

Eleven

While working an evening at the shop
Luna came to stumble upon a book,
To raise the dead,
It turned her head,
To think that maybe her grief could stop.

Twelve

Down deep into the
Earth, gather soil, wriggly worms.
And far into
The woods; pine needles everlast.
Heart, taken from a faerie:
It must
Still beat.
Now place these in the mouth,
Of the body you wish
To bring back.
Then be sure to
Have a set of candles
Encircling your love.
Enter at your own risk.
Now say the words to raise the
Dead.
Bring them back from
Underground. Let
Them
Live with us once more.
It is not the end
For them.
Everlast, hand-in-hand;
It is your time to
Shine together again.

Thirteen

Dust settles,
Light fades.
Night always
Arrives, remember?

"Luna, where
Are you
Going? Is
Everything okay?"

Silence is
Her voice.
It guides
Her to

The Woods.

Fourteen

Branches littering the ground.
Starlight against frost
Glitters like an endless sky

No Will-o-the-wisps appear;
Tonight they will not
Guide, for her heart beats so cold.

They watch from beyond the trees,
Make no move to stop.
Mistakes are made for making.

Fifteen

Clouds cover the moon,
Descending her in darkness.
So deep the shadows loom.

On a tree is carved a rune,
To protect from the heartless.
Clouds cover the moon.

In the distance is a tune;
Her eyes widen with alertness.
So deep the shadows loom.

There are soggy leaves strewn
On the forest floor, regardless.
Clouds cover the moon.

The faeries cower and swoon,
But one who hovers; fearless.
So deep the shadows loom.

Oh the sound of a faery's croon.
The knife cuts with a harshness.
Clouds cover the moon;
So deep the shadows loom.

Sixteen

She's in the cemetery
She digs through the earth,
And prises open the coffin.

Worms and dirt, pine needles; heart.
There's blood on her hands.
Her fingers open the mouth.

Chemicals, formaldehyde,
And death in her nose.
She readies the body now.

The candles, how they flicker.
How the night is dark.
How her words stumble, stutter.

But the dirt around her stirs,
The air gets colder;
The flames - now pillars of smoke.

And a groan comes from the ground.
Pan stands before her.
And oh. Oh! They are a sight.

Seventeen

Science and magic;
So different;
So similar.
Frankenstein brought
His pieces together,
Let the lightning spark!
"It's alive!" He cries,
Before the doubt
Sets in. Oh God, what
Has he done?
This is no Adam laid
Out before him.
This is a creature.
Monster.
Abomination.
Repent! Repent!
For life is not
For playing with.
As Adam squeezes
With his hands,
A strength unrivaled.
For death *is* for
Playing with.

Eighteen

Regret slices right through
Luna's fragile heart.
This is not the Pan she knew;
The Pan who was funny, kind, smart.

Now she sees why it is taboo,
To treat dark magic as an art.
Maybe death is supposed to come
And tear everything apart.

When *Pan* runs she must pursue
With a leap and a dart
The knife cuts right through.
She watches *Pan*'s second life depart.

To the truth she must succumb;
Let her hands release the knife.
Oh how she feels so dumb
To think she could control life.

Nineteen

Pan's body in her arms.
Though Pan's lips are theirs
They will never smile again.
Luna pushes up the corners
With her fingers. Cringes,
As Pan's stiff cheeks
Crumple. How she wishes
They would smile again.
That she could see their smile
Again.
She lays their body in
The coffin, shuts the lid
Tight, but not before she
Reclaims the remains of
A faery's heart - another
who will not smile again.
One shovel at a time,
She buries her friend
With calloused hands.
Maybe, one day, she
Will smile again.

Twenty

The witch went back through the wood;
Retraced her steps from before,
When things were bad and things were good.
Before she had entered through that door;
When she mistook could with should.
From a time when she felt so sure.
When the pine needles crunched beneath her feet
And the bonfire sparked despite the sleet.

And now she has returned to the fire,
To bring back the ancient faery's remains;
The bonfire: now a funeral pyre.
Forest animals come to release their pain,
Their cries are the song of a mourning choir.
But they do not need Luna to explain,
For grief is something they all have felt;
And all must go through the loss they're dealt.

Twenty-One

Owl hoots turn to birdsong.
Glittering cobwebs go out of view.
Squirrels and mice scramble along,
Socks turn soggy from grass dew.
A bluebell sprouts from the earth;
A periwinkle blue to match the lightening sky.
And sunflowers turn to see the day's rebirth.
Through tree branches the breeze does sigh.

Luna sits on the cool, damp grass
To watch a new Sun as it does arise.
"Why?" She sobs, "must time still pass?"
And oh how the young witch cries.
Grief, loss, regret. She's got it all inside
But there's hope, too, on a coming tide.

ACKNOWLEDGEMENT

Thank you to my mum, for putting up with me more than I wish she'd have to, and for her supporting me and my creative endeavours. I'd also like to thank my older sister, Catherine, for getting me into writing. It's our thing now; as well as rambling aimlessly about books.
Special thanks to my twin, for often being the first to understand.
Thank you to Simon, my fateful friend, who helped me to create the characters Luna and Pan. I hope to explore their friendship more in the future - and help bring better representation of queer platonic partnerships!
And also thank you to my dogs. They can't read this but I'm including them anyway. Halle is a great armrest, and Andie loves to snuggle under my arms when I'm trying to type, and I wouldn't want them any other way... except maybe a little more quiet.
Lastly, thank you to anyone who reads this! It would mean a lot for this to be enjoyed.

www.ingramcontent.com/pod-product-compliance
Lightning Source LLC
LaVergne TN
LVHW021350200726

843509LV00014B/2777